MW01622282

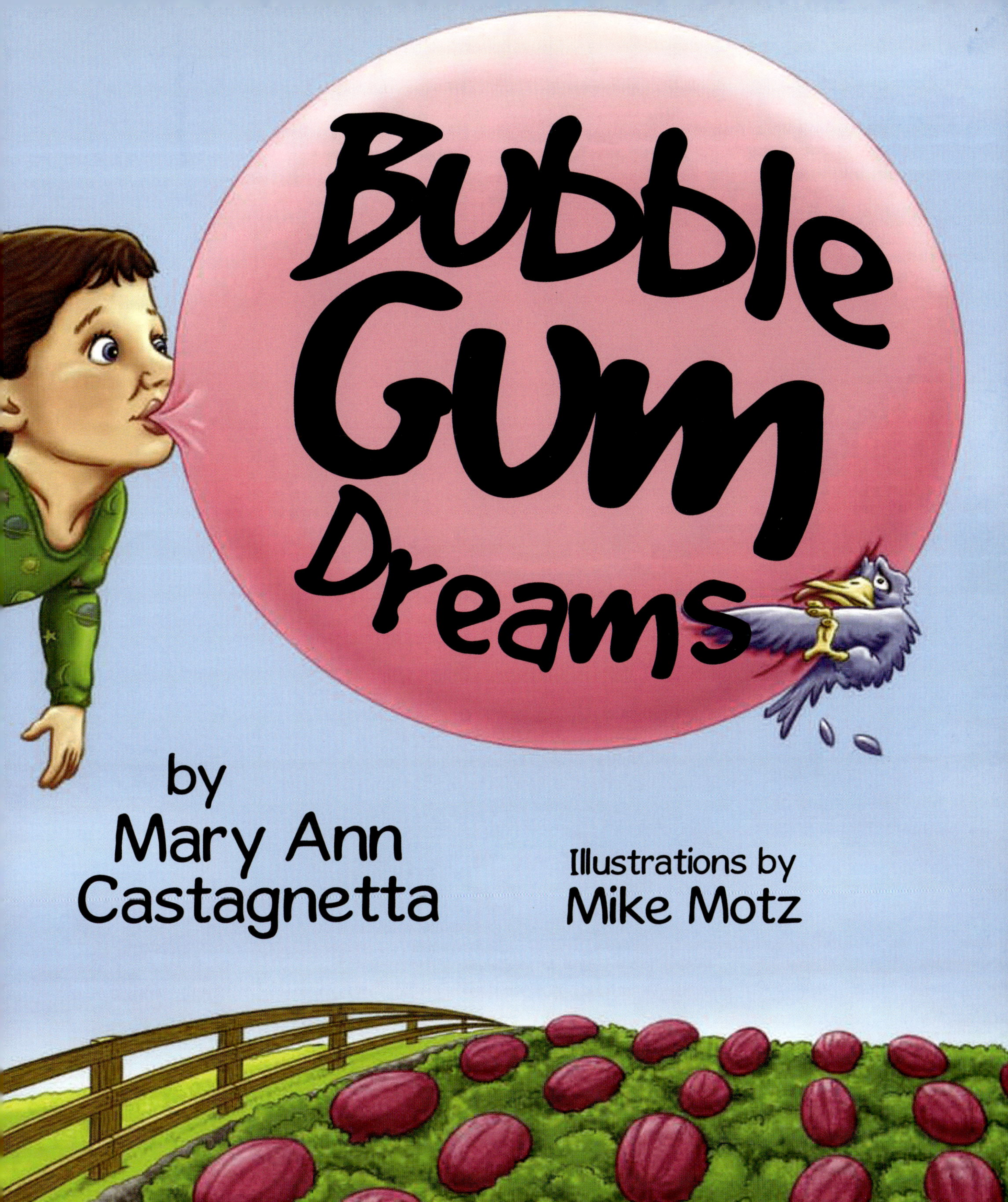
Bubble Gum Dreams
by
Mary Ann Castagnetta
Illustrations by
Mike Motz

Published in the United States of America by Elephant Soup, LLC., 2017

Library of Congress Cataloging-in-Publication Data

ISBN: 978-0-9842145-0-1

Fourth Printing — 2017

Third Printing — 2013

Second Printing — 2010

First Printing — 2009

BUBBLE GUM DREAMS

Author — Mary Ann Castagnetta

Illustrator — Mike Motz

Website: www.maryanncastagnetta.com

" I Wish You Bubble Gum Dreams!"

PRINTED IN THE UNITED STATES OF AMERICA

This book was inspired by,
and is dedicated to my son,
John,
who has
Bubble Gum Dreams
every night.

After dinner was John's favorite part of the day.
He loved to play in the bathtub with all of his tub toys.

He loved when his Mom dried him off
and wrapped the big, warm towel around him.

He loved getting into his favorite pajamas.

After getting into his pajamas,
John would sit with his Mom
in a big stuffed chair
as she read to him.
He would twirl his hair between
his fingers and drink his milk
while his Mom made the stories
so funny, the milk would almost
come out of his nose

He loved when his Mom tucked him
into bed, kissed him on his
forehead and whispered in his ear
"Good night my little boy.
I love you."
On this one particular night,
John's Mom whispered
something new to him.
She said, "Good night my little boy.
I love you.
I wish you Bubble Gum Dreams."

John laughed and asked, “Mom, what are
Bubble Gum Dreams?”
“Why”, she said, Bubble Gum Dreams are dreams that are just like bubble gum. They are sweet, and fun, and very, very pink.”

As his Mom left his room,
John closed his eyes and soon was fast asleep, all the time remembering his Mom's words.
That night, John had the sweetest, most fun dream he had ever had.

In his dream he was walking in a big field of flowers,
all different shades of pink.
And the sun wasn't yellow, but a beautiful, shining, pink globe.

As he walked through the field, John could see
a flock of pink birds flying in the distance,
as pretty, pink bunny rabbits hopped all around.

Up ahead, John could see a group of children playing in a circle.
They were laughing, and singing and dancing.
"Hi, my name is John", he said.
"Hi John", the children replied. "Won't you play with us?"

"We're taking turns to see who can blow the biggest bubble.
Here's a piece of bubble gum. Why don't you have a try?"
"Okay" said John. John chewed the gum
till it was just the right texture for blowing bubbles.
Then he began to blow.

The bubble got bigger and
bigger and bigger,
until it was so big
it lifted him off the ground
like a giant balloon.

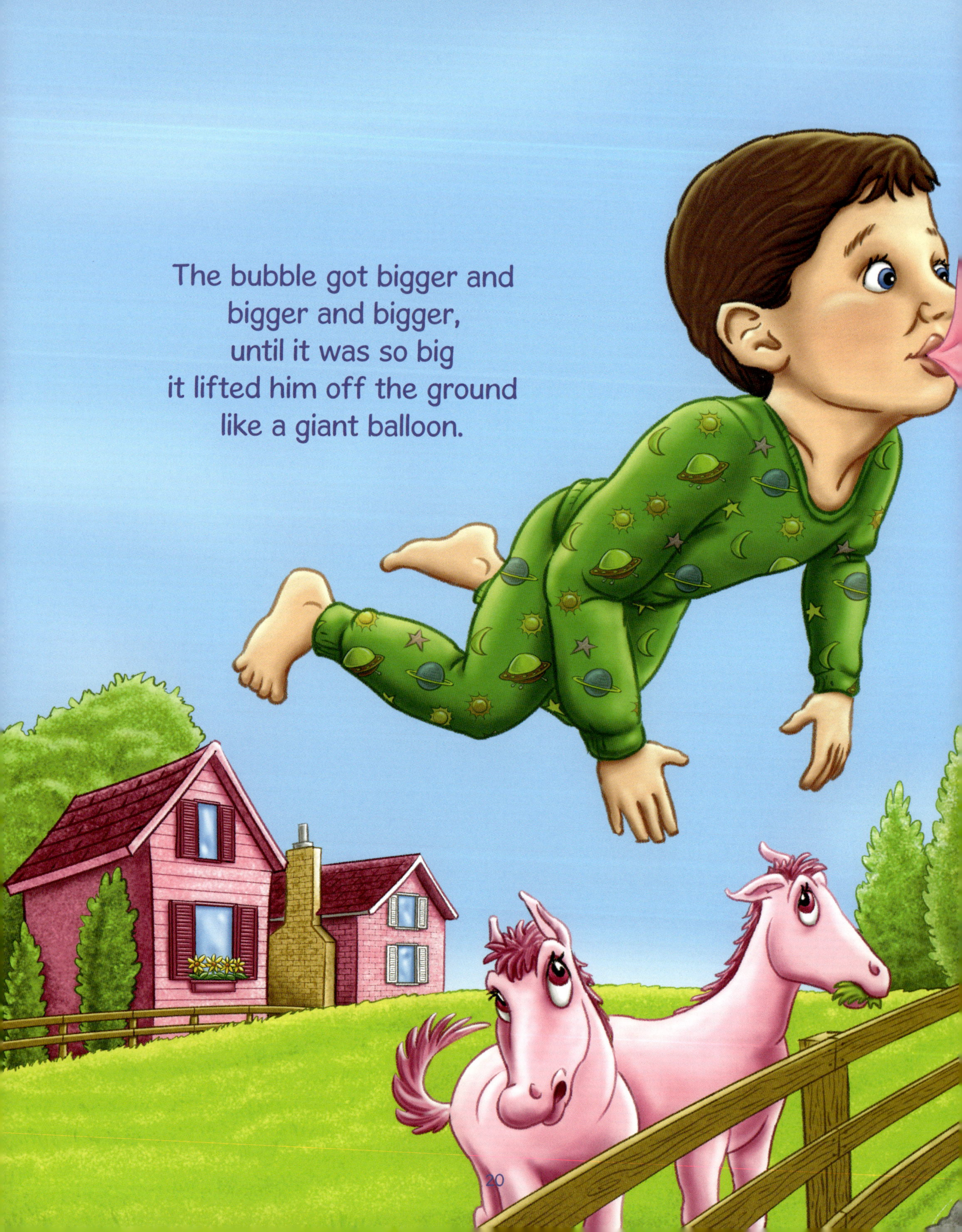

Before he knew it, John was flying!
Flying over pink houses, and pink horses
and rows of pink melons.

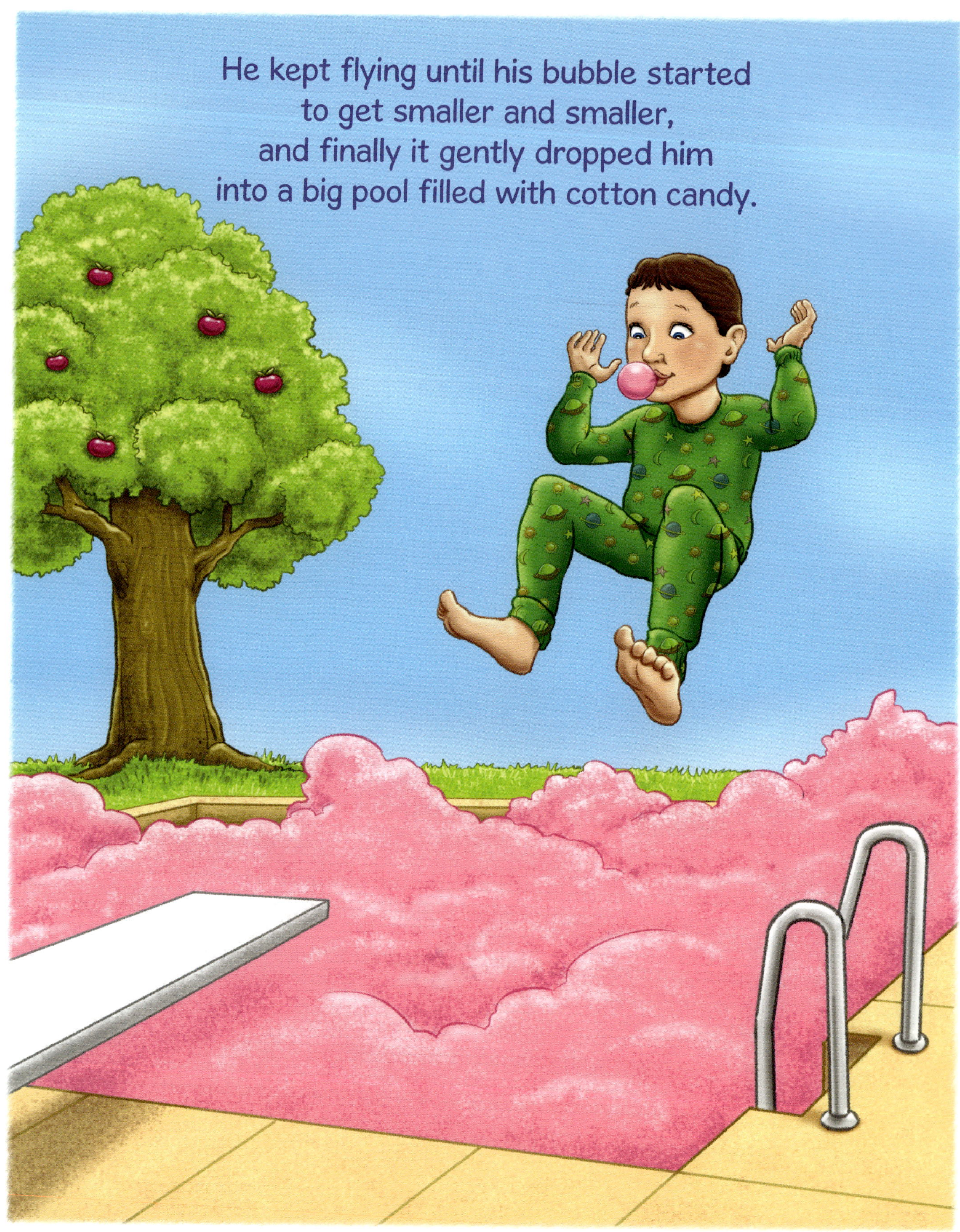
He kept flying until his bubble started
to get smaller and smaller,
and finally it gently dropped him
into a big pool filled with cotton candy.

He began eating the cotton candy.
It was the sweetest and most delicious candy he had ever tasted.
When he ate all the cotton candy
his belly could hold, he climbed out of the pool.

Once out of the pool, he found himself standing
in front of a pink door.
He opened the door, and what do you think he
found? It was his bedroom!

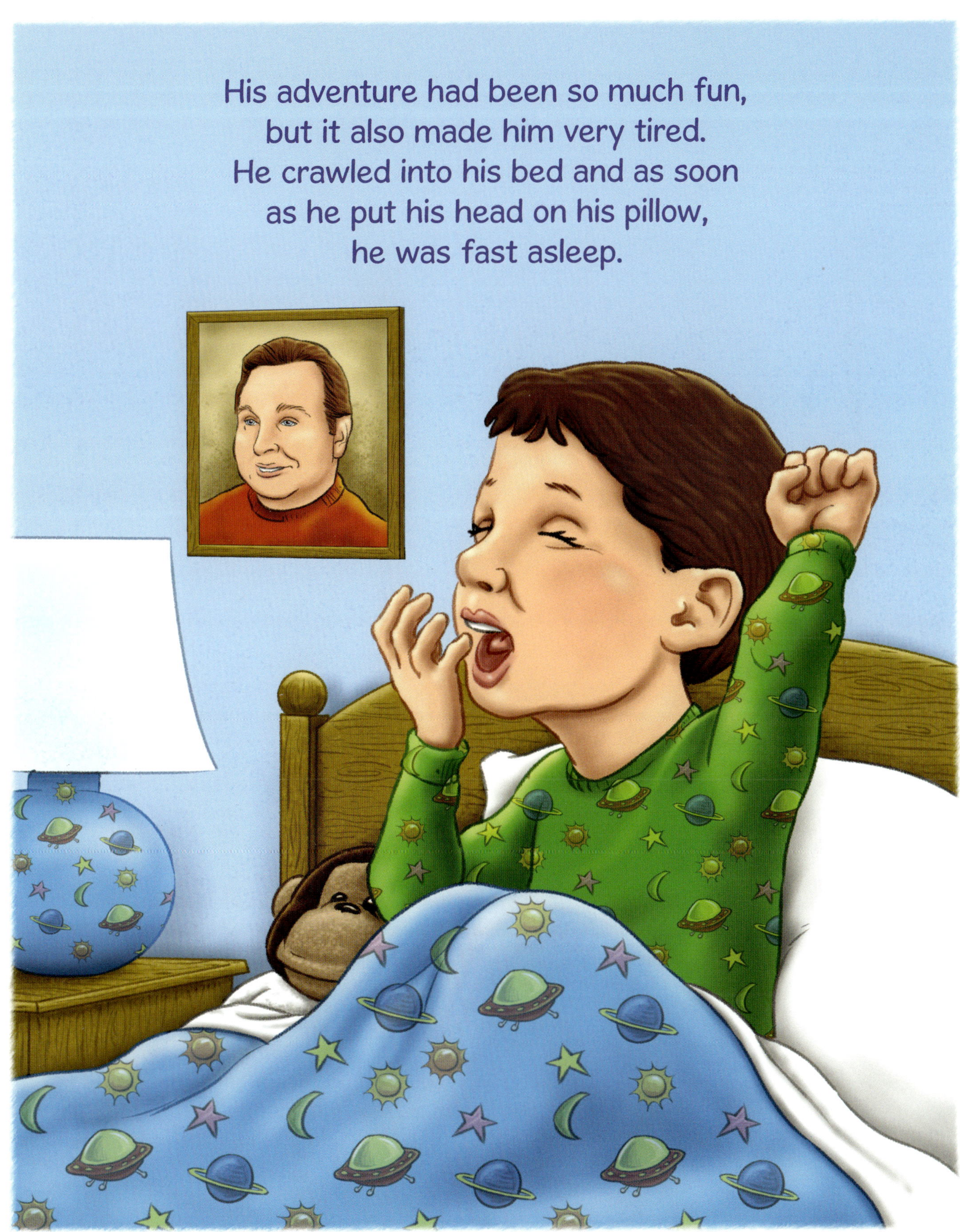

His adventure had been so much fun,
but it also made him very tired.
He crawled into his bed and as soon
as he put his head on his pillow,
he was fast asleep.

The next morning when John awoke,
he couldn't wait to tell his Mom all about his dream.
He jumped out of bed and ran into the kitchen
where he knew his Mom was making breakfast.

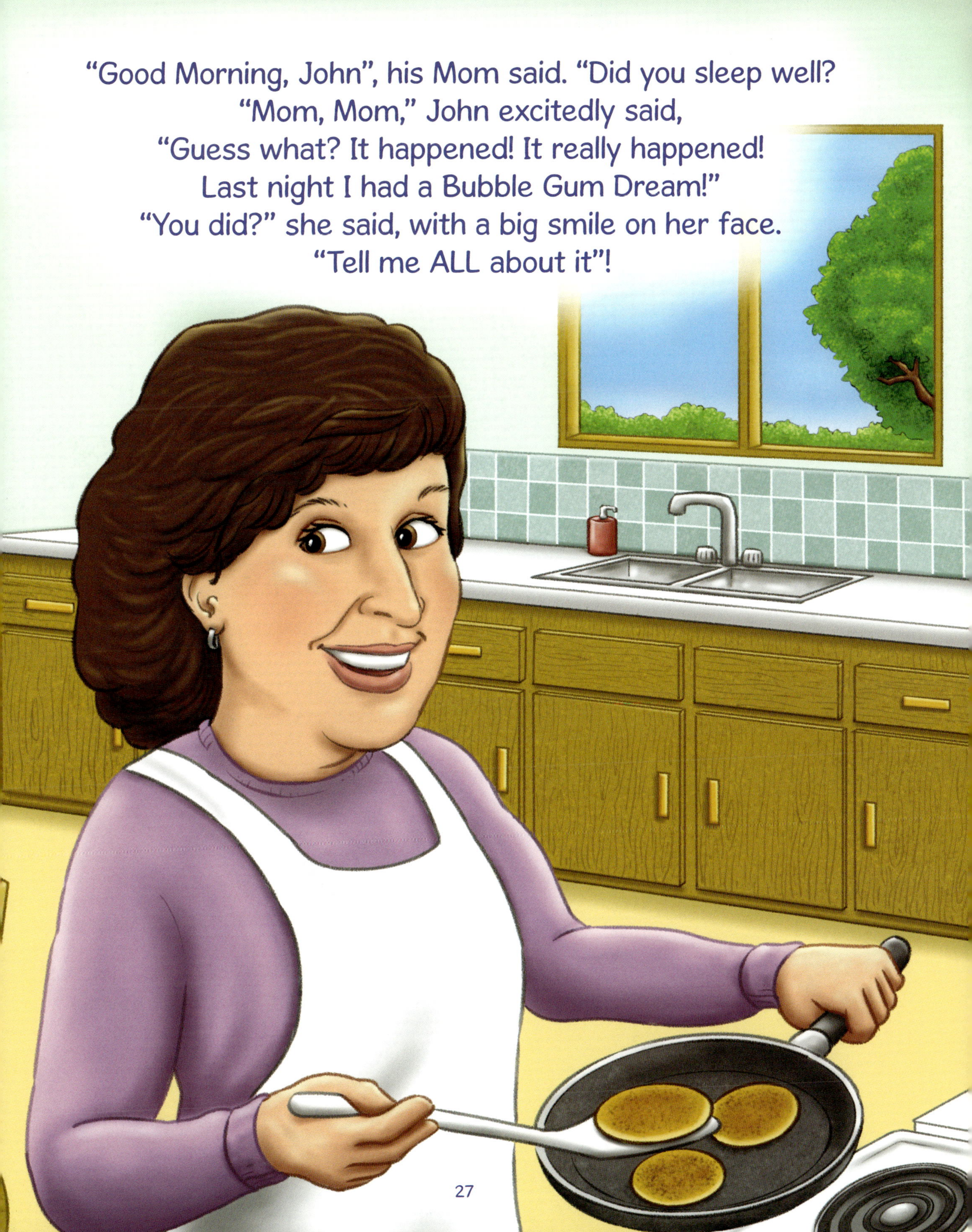

"Good Morning, John", his Mom said. "Did you sleep well?
"Mom, Mom," John excitedly said,
"Guess what? It happened! It really happened!
Last night I had a Bubble Gum Dream!"
"You did?" she said, with a big smile on her face.
"Tell me ALL about it"!

As John started to tell his Mom his dream, she noticed something in his ear. "What is this?" asked his Mom. To his amazement she pulled a piece of pink cotton candy out of his ear!

John and his Mom both giggled and giggled
all through breakfast as John told her
about his exciting Bubble Gum Dream.

The End

Tremendous Love and Thanks to my wonderful husband, Eddie. As always, he is my rock, and without his unconditional love, support and encouragement, Bubble Gum Dreams would have never been possible.